THIS BOOK BELONGS TO :

WEBSITE :

USERNAME :

PASSWORD :

NOTE :

WEBSITE :

USERNAME :

PASSWORD :

NOTE :

WEBSITE :

USERNAME :

PASSWORD :

NOTE :

WEBSITE :

USERNAME :

PASSWORD :

NOTE :

A

WEBSITE :

USERNAME :

PASSWORD :

NOTE :

WEBSITE :

USERNAME :

PASSWORD :

NOTE :

WEBSITE :

USERNAME :

PASSWORD :

NOTE :

WEBSITE :

USERNAME :

PASSWORD :

NOTE :

WEBSITE :

USERNAME :

PASSWORD :

NOTE :

WEBSITE :

USERNAME :

PASSWORD :

NOTE :

WEBSITE :

USERNAME :

PASSWORD :

NOTE :

WEBSITE :

USERNAME :

PASSWORD :

NOTE :

A

WEBSITE :

USERNAME :

PASSWORD :

NOTE :

WEBSITE :

USERNAME :

PASSWORD :

NOTE :

WEBSITE :

USERNAME :

PASSWORD :

NOTE :

WEBSITE :

USERNAME :

PASSWORD :

NOTE :

WEBSITE :

USERNAME :

PASSWORD :

NOTE :

WEBSITE :

USERNAME :

PASSWORD :

NOTE :

WEBSITE :

USERNAME :

PASSWORD :

NOTE :

WEBSITE :

USERNAME :

PASSWORD :

NOTE :

B

WEBSITE :

USERNAME :

PASSWORD :

NOTE :

WEBSITE :

USERNAME :

PASSWORD :

NOTE :

WEBSITE :

USERNAME :

PASSWORD :

NOTE :

WEBSITE :

USERNAME :

PASSWORD :

NOTE :

WEBSITE :

USERNAME :

PASSWORD :

NOTE :

WEBSITE :

USERNAME :

PASSWORD :

NOTE :

WEBSITE :

USERNAME :

PASSWORD :

NOTE :

WEBSITE :

USERNAME :

PASSWORD :

NOTE :

B

WEBSITE :

USERNAME :

PASSWORD :

NOTE :

WEBSITE :

USERNAME :

PASSWORD :

NOTE :

WEBSITE :

USERNAME :

PASSWORD :

NOTE :

WEBSITE :

USERNAME :

PASSWORD :

NOTE :

WEBSITE :

USERNAME :

PASSWORD :

NOTE :

//

WEBSITE :

USERNAME :

PASSWORD :

NOTE :

//

WEBSITE :

USERNAME :

PASSWORD :

NOTE :

//

WEBSITE :

USERNAME :

PASSWORD :

NOTE :

//

C

WEBSITE :

USERNAME :

PASSWORD :

NOTE :

WEBSITE :

USERNAME :

PASSWORD :

NOTE :

WEBSITE :

USERNAME :

PASSWORD :

NOTE :

WEBSITE :

USERNAME :

PASSWORD :

NOTE :

WEBSITE :

USERNAME :

PASSWORD :

NOTE :

WEBSITE :

USERNAME :

PASSWORD :

NOTE :

WEBSITE :

USERNAME :

PASSWORD :

NOTE :

WEBSITE :

USERNAME :

PASSWORD :

NOTE :

WEBSITE :

USERNAME :

PASSWORD :

NOTE :

C

//

WEBSITE :

USERNAME :

PASSWORD :

NOTE :

//

WEBSITE :

USERNAME :

PASSWORD :

NOTE :

//

WEBSITE :

USERNAME :

PASSWORD :

NOTE :

//

WEBSITE :

USERNAME :

PASSWORD :

NOTE :

WEBSITE :

USERNAME :

PASSWORD :

NOTE :

WEBSITE :

USERNAME :

PASSWORD :

NOTE :

WEBSITE :

USERNAME :

PASSWORD :

NOTE :

D

WEBSITE :

USERNAME :

PASSWORD :

NOTE :

WEBSITE :

USERNAME :

PASSWORD :

NOTE :

WEBSITE :

USERNAME :

PASSWORD :

NOTE :

WEBSITE :

USERNAME :

PASSWORD :

NOTE :

WEBSITE :

USERNAME :

PASSWORD :

NOTE :

WEBSITE :

USERNAME :

PASSWORD :

NOTE :

WEBSITE :

USERNAME :

PASSWORD :

NOTE :

WEBSITE :

USERNAME :

PASSWORD :

NOTE :

D

WEBSITE :

USERNAME :

PASSWORD :

NOTE :

WEBSITE :

USERNAME :

PASSWORD :

NOTE :

WEBSITE :

USERNAME :

PASSWORD :

NOTE :

WEBSITE :

USERNAME :

PASSWORD :

NOTE :

WEBSITE :

USERNAME :

PASSWORD :

NOTE :

//

WEBSITE :

USERNAME :

PASSWORD :

NOTE :

//

WEBSITE :

USERNAME :

PASSWORD :

NOTE :

//

WEBSITE :

USERNAME :

PASSWORD :

NOTE :

//

E

WEBSITE :

USERNAME :

PASSWORD :

NOTE :

WEBSITE :

USERNAME :

PASSWORD :

NOTE :

WEBSITE :

USERNAME :

PASSWORD :

NOTE :

WEBSITE :

USERNAME :

PASSWORD :

NOTE :

WEBSITE :

USERNAME :

PASSWORD :

NOTE :

WEBSITE :

USERNAME :

PASSWORD :

NOTE :

WEBSITE :

USERNAME :

PASSWORD :

NOTE :

WEBSITE :

USERNAME :

PASSWORD :

NOTE :

E

WEBSITE :

USERNAME :

PASSWORD :

NOTE :

WEBSITE :

USERNAME :

PASSWORD :

NOTE :

WEBSITE :

USERNAME :

PASSWORD :

NOTE :

WEBSITE :

USERNAME :

PASSWORD :

NOTE :

WEBSITE :

USERNAME :

PASSWORD :

NOTE :

WEBSITE :

USERNAME :

PASSWORD :

NOTE :

WEBSITE :

USERNAME :

PASSWORD :

NOTE :

WEBSITE :

USERNAME :

PASSWORD :

NOTE :

F

WEBSITE :

USERNAME :

PASSWORD :

NOTE :

WEBSITE :

USERNAME :

PASSWORD :

NOTE :

WEBSITE :

USERNAME :

PASSWORD :

NOTE :

WEBSITE :

USERNAME :

PASSWORD :

NOTE :

WEBSITE :

USERNAME :

PASSWORD :

NOTE :

WEBSITE :

USERNAME :

PASSWORD :

NOTE :

WEBSITE :

USERNAME :

PASSWORD :

NOTE :

WEBSITE :

USERNAME :

PASSWORD :

NOTE :

F

WEBSITE :

USERNAME :

PASSWORD :

NOTE :

WEBSITE :

USERNAME :

PASSWORD :

NOTE :

WEBSITE :

USERNAME :

PASSWORD :

NOTE :

WEBSITE :

USERNAME :

PASSWORD :

NOTE :

WEBSITE :

USERNAME :

PASSWORD :

NOTE :

WEBSITE :

USERNAME :

PASSWORD :

NOTE :

WEBSITE :

USERNAME :

PASSWORD :

NOTE :

WEBSITE :

USERNAME :

PASSWORD :

NOTE :

G

WEBSITE :

USERNAME :

PASSWORD :

NOTE :

WEBSITE :

USERNAME :

PASSWORD :

NOTE :

WEBSITE :

USERNAME :

PASSWORD :

NOTE :

WEBSITE :

USERNAME :

PASSWORD :

NOTE :

WEBSITE :

USERNAME :

PASSWORD :

NOTE :

//

WEBSITE :

USERNAME :

PASSWORD :

NOTE :

//

WEBSITE :

USERNAME :

PASSWORD :

NOTE :

//

WEBSITE :

USERNAME :

PASSWORD :

NOTE :

//

G

WEBSITE :

USERNAME :

PASSWORD :

NOTE :

WEBSITE :

USERNAME :

PASSWORD :

NOTE :

WEBSITE :

USERNAME :

PASSWORD :

NOTE :

WEBSITE :

USERNAME :

PASSWORD :

NOTE :

WEBSITE :

USERNAME :

PASSWORD :

NOTE :

WEBSITE :

USERNAME :

PASSWORD :

NOTE :

WEBSITE :

USERNAME :

PASSWORD :

NOTE :

WEBSITE :

USERNAME :

PASSWORD :

NOTE :

H

WEBSITE :

USERNAME :

PASSWORD :

NOTE :

WEBSITE :

USERNAME :

PASSWORD :

NOTE :

WEBSITE :

USERNAME :

PASSWORD :

NOTE :

WEBSITE :

USERNAME :

PASSWORD :

NOTE :

WEBSITE :

USERNAME :

PASSWORD :

NOTE :

WEBSITE :

USERNAME :

PASSWORD :

NOTE :

WEBSITE :

USERNAME :

PASSWORD :

NOTE :

WEBSITE :

USERNAME :

PASSWORD :

NOTE :

H

WEBSITE :

USERNAME :

PASSWORD :

NOTE :

WEBSITE :

USERNAME :

PASSWORD :

NOTE :

WEBSITE :

USERNAME :

PASSWORD :

NOTE :

WEBSITE :

USERNAME :

PASSWORD :

NOTE :

WEBSITE :

USERNAME :

PASSWORD :

NOTE :

WEBSITE :

USERNAME :

PASSWORD :

NOTE :

WEBSITE :

USERNAME :

PASSWORD :

NOTE :

WEBSITE :

USERNAME :

PASSWORD :

NOTE :

I

WEBSITE :

USERNAME :

PASSWORD :

NOTE :

WEBSITE :

USERNAME :

PASSWORD :

NOTE :

WEBSITE :

USERNAME :

PASSWORD :

NOTE :

WEBSITE :

USERNAME :

PASSWORD :

NOTE :

WEBSITE :

USERNAME :

PASSWORD :

NOTE :

WEBSITE :

USERNAME :

PASSWORD :

NOTE :

WEBSITE :

USERNAME :

PASSWORD :

NOTE :

WEBSITE :

USERNAME :

PASSWORD :

NOTE :

I

WEBSITE :

USERNAME :

PASSWORD :

NOTE :

WEBSITE :

USERNAME :

PASSWORD :

NOTE :

WEBSITE :

USERNAME :

PASSWORD :

NOTE :

WEBSITE :

USERNAME :

PASSWORD :

NOTE :

WEBSITE :

USERNAME :

PASSWORD :

NOTE :

WEBSITE :

USERNAME :

PASSWORD :

NOTE :

WEBSITE :

USERNAME :

PASSWORD :

NOTE :

WEBSITE :

USERNAME :

PASSWORD :

NOTE :

J

WEBSITE :

USERNAME :

PASSWORD :

NOTE :

WEBSITE :

USERNAME :

PASSWORD :

NOTE :

WEBSITE :

USERNAME :

PASSWORD :

NOTE :

WEBSITE :

USERNAME :

PASSWORD :

NOTE :

WEBSITE :

USERNAME :

PASSWORD :

NOTE :

WEBSITE :

USERNAME :

PASSWORD :

NOTE :

WEBSITE :

USERNAME :

PASSWORD :

NOTE :

WEBSITE :

USERNAME :

PASSWORD :

NOTE :

J

WEBSITE :

USERNAME :

PASSWORD :

NOTE :

WEBSITE :

USERNAME :

PASSWORD :

NOTE :

WEBSITE :

USERNAME :

PASSWORD :

NOTE :

WEBSITE :

USERNAME :

PASSWORD :

NOTE :

WEBSITE :

USERNAME :

PASSWORD :

NOTE :

WEBSITE :

USERNAME :

PASSWORD :

NOTE :

WEBSITE :

USERNAME :

PASSWORD :

NOTE :

WEBSITE :

USERNAME :

PASSWORD :

NOTE :

K

WEBSITE :

USERNAME :

PASSWORD :

NOTE :

WEBSITE :

USERNAME :

PASSWORD :

NOTE :

WEBSITE :

USERNAME :

PASSWORD :

NOTE :

WEBSITE :

USERNAME :

PASSWORD :

NOTE :

WEBSITE :

USERNAME :

PASSWORD :

NOTE :

//

WEBSITE :

USERNAME :

PASSWORD :

NOTE :

//

WEBSITE :

USERNAME :

PASSWORD :

NOTE :

//

WEBSITE :

USERNAME :

PASSWORD :

NOTE :

//

K

WEBSITE :

USERNAME :

PASSWORD :

NOTE :

//

WEBSITE :

USERNAME :

PASSWORD :

NOTE :

//

WEBSITE :

USERNAME :

PASSWORD :

NOTE :

//

WEBSITE :

USERNAME :

PASSWORD :

NOTE :

//

WEBSITE :

USERNAME :

PASSWORD :

NOTE :

WEBSITE :

USERNAME :

PASSWORD :

NOTE :

WEBSITE :

USERNAME :

PASSWORD :

NOTE :

WEBSITE :

USERNAME :

PASSWORD :

NOTE :

L

WEBSITE :

USERNAME :

PASSWORD :

NOTE :

WEBSITE :

USERNAME :

PASSWORD :

NOTE :

WEBSITE :

USERNAME :

PASSWORD :

NOTE :

WEBSITE :

USERNAME :

PASSWORD :

NOTE :

WEBSITE :

USERNAME :

PASSWORD :

NOTE :

WEBSITE :

USERNAME :

PASSWORD :

NOTE :

WEBSITE :

USERNAME :

PASSWORD :

NOTE :

WEBSITE :

USERNAME :

PASSWORD :

NOTE :

WEBSITE :

USERNAME :

PASSWORD :

NOTE :

L

WEBSITE :

USERNAME :

PASSWORD :

NOTE :

WEBSITE :

USERNAME :

PASSWORD :

NOTE :

WEBSITE :

USERNAME :

PASSWORD :

NOTE :

WEBSITE :

USERNAME :

PASSWORD :

NOTE :

//

WEBSITE :

USERNAME :

PASSWORD :

NOTE :

//

WEBSITE :

USERNAME :

PASSWORD :

NOTE :

//

WEBSITE :

USERNAME :

PASSWORD :

NOTE :

//

M

WEBSITE :

USERNAME :

PASSWORD :

NOTE :

WEBSITE :

USERNAME :

PASSWORD :

NOTE :

WEBSITE :

USERNAME :

PASSWORD :

NOTE :

WEBSITE :

USERNAME :

PASSWORD :

NOTE :

WEBSITE :

USERNAME :

PASSWORD :

NOTE :

//

WEBSITE :

USERNAME :

PASSWORD :

NOTE :

//

WEBSITE :

USERNAME :

PASSWORD :

NOTE :

//

WEBSITE :

USERNAME :

PASSWORD :

NOTE :

//

M

WEBSITE :

USERNAME :

PASSWORD :

NOTE :

//

WEBSITE :

USERNAME :

PASSWORD :

NOTE :

//

WEBSITE :

USERNAME :

PASSWORD :

NOTE :

//

WEBSITE :

USERNAME :

PASSWORD :

NOTE :

//

WEBSITE :

USERNAME :

PASSWORD :

NOTE :

WEBSITE :

USERNAME :

PASSWORD :

NOTE :

WEBSITE :

USERNAME :

PASSWORD :

NOTE :

WEBSITE :

USERNAME :

PASSWORD :

NOTE :

N

WEBSITE :

USERNAME :

PASSWORD :

NOTE :

WEBSITE :

USERNAME :

PASSWORD :

NOTE :

WEBSITE :

USERNAME :

PASSWORD :

NOTE :

WEBSITE :

USERNAME :

PASSWORD :

NOTE :

WEBSITE :

USERNAME :

PASSWORD :

NOTE :

WEBSITE :

USERNAME :

PASSWORD :

NOTE :

WEBSITE :

USERNAME :

PASSWORD :

NOTE :

WEBSITE :

USERNAME :

PASSWORD :

NOTE :

N

WEBSITE :

USERNAME :

PASSWORD :

NOTE :

WEBSITE :

USERNAME :

PASSWORD :

NOTE :

WEBSITE :

USERNAME :

PASSWORD :

NOTE :

WEBSITE :

USERNAME :

PASSWORD :

NOTE :

WEBSITE :

USERNAME :

PASSWORD :

NOTE :

//

WEBSITE :

USERNAME :

PASSWORD :

NOTE :

//

WEBSITE :

USERNAME :

PASSWORD :

NOTE :

//

WEBSITE :

USERNAME :

PASSWORD :

NOTE :

//

O

WEBSITE :

USERNAME :

PASSWORD :

NOTE :

WEBSITE :

USERNAME :

PASSWORD :

NOTE :

WEBSITE :

USERNAME :

PASSWORD :

NOTE :

WEBSITE :

USERNAME :

PASSWORD :

NOTE :

WEBSITE :

USERNAME :

PASSWORD :

NOTE :

WEBSITE :

USERNAME :

PASSWORD :

NOTE :

WEBSITE :

USERNAME :

PASSWORD :

NOTE :

WEBSITE :

USERNAME :

PASSWORD :

NOTE :

O

WEBSITE :

USERNAME :

PASSWORD :

NOTE :

WEBSITE :

USERNAME :

PASSWORD :

NOTE :

WEBSITE :

USERNAME :

PASSWORD :

NOTE :

WEBSITE :

USERNAME :

PASSWORD :

NOTE :

WEBSITE :

USERNAME :

PASSWORD :

NOTE :

WEBSITE :

USERNAME :

PASSWORD :

NOTE :

WEBSITE :

USERNAME :

PASSWORD :

NOTE :

WEBSITE :

USERNAME :

PASSWORD :

NOTE :

P

WEBSITE :

USERNAME :

PASSWORD :

NOTE :

WEBSITE :

USERNAME :

PASSWORD :

NOTE :

WEBSITE :

USERNAME :

PASSWORD :

NOTE :

WEBSITE :

USERNAME :

PASSWORD :

NOTE :

WEBSITE :

USERNAME :

PASSWORD :

NOTE :

WEBSITE :

USERNAME :

PASSWORD :

NOTE :

WEBSITE :

USERNAME :

PASSWORD :

NOTE :

WEBSITE :

USERNAME :

PASSWORD :

NOTE :

P

WEBSITE :

USERNAME :

PASSWORD :

NOTE :

//

WEBSITE :

USERNAME :

PASSWORD :

NOTE :

//

WEBSITE :

USERNAME :

PASSWORD :

NOTE :

//

WEBSITE :

USERNAME :

PASSWORD :

NOTE :

//

WEBSITE :

USERNAME :

PASSWORD :

NOTE :

//

WEBSITE :

USERNAME :

PASSWORD :

NOTE :

//

WEBSITE :

USERNAME :

PASSWORD :

NOTE :

//

WEBSITE :

USERNAME :

PASSWORD :

NOTE :

//

Q

WEBSITE :

USERNAME :

PASSWORD :

NOTE :

WEBSITE :

USERNAME :

PASSWORD :

NOTE :

WEBSITE :

USERNAME :

PASSWORD :

NOTE :

WEBSITE :

USERNAME :

PASSWORD :

NOTE :

WEBSITE :

USERNAME :

PASSWORD :

NOTE :

WEBSITE :

USERNAME :

PASSWORD :

NOTE :

WEBSITE :

USERNAME :

PASSWORD :

NOTE :

WEBSITE :

USERNAME :

PASSWORD :

NOTE :

Q

WEBSITE :

USERNAME :

PASSWORD :

NOTE :

WEBSITE :

USERNAME :

PASSWORD :

NOTE :

WEBSITE :

USERNAME :

PASSWORD :

NOTE :

WEBSITE :

USERNAME :

PASSWORD :

NOTE :

WEBSITE :

USERNAME ;

PASSWORD :

NOTE :

//

WEBSITE :

USERNAME :

PASSWORD :

NOTE :

//

WEBSITE :

USERNAME :

PASSWORD :

NOTE :

//

WEBSITE :

USERNAME :

PASSWORD :

NOTE :

//

R

WEBSITE :

USERNAME :

PASSWORD :

NOTE :

WEBSITE :

USERNAME :

PASSWORD :

NOTE :

WEBSITE :

USERNAME :

PASSWORD :

NOTE :

WEBSITE :

USERNAME :

PASSWORD :

NOTE :

WEBSITE :

USERNAME :

PASSWORD :

NOTE :

WEBSITE :

USERNAME :

PASSWORD :

NOTE :

WEBSITE :

USERNAME :

PASSWORD :

NOTE :

WEBSITE :

USERNAME :

PASSWORD :

NOTE :

R

WEBSITE :

USERNAME :

PASSWORD :

NOTE :

WEBSITE :

USERNAME :

PASSWORD :

NOTE :

WEBSITE :

USERNAME :

PASSWORD :

NOTE :

WEBSITE :

USERNAME :

PASSWORD :

NOTE :

WEBSITE :

USERNAME :

PASSWORD :

NOTE :

WEBSITE :

USERNAME :

PASSWORD :

NOTE :

WEBSITE :

USERNAME :

PASSWORD :

NOTE :

WEBSITE :

USERNAME :

PASSWORD :

NOTE :

S

WEBSITE :

USERNAME :

PASSWORD :

NOTE :

//

WEBSITE :

USERNAME :

PASSWORD :

NOTE :

//

WEBSITE :

USERNAME :

PASSWORD :

NOTE :

//

WEBSITE :

USERNAME :

PASSWORD :

NOTE :

//

WEBSITE :

USERNAME :

PASSWORD :

NOTE :

//

WEBSITE :

USERNAME :

PASSWORD :

NOTE :

//

WEBSITE :

USERNAME :

PASSWORD :

NOTE :

//

WEBSITE :

USERNAME :

PASSWORD :

NOTE :

//

S

WEBSITE :

USERNAME :

PASSWORD :

NOTE :

WEBSITE :

USERNAME :

PASSWORD :

NOTE :

WEBSITE :

USERNAME :

PASSWORD :

NOTE :

WEBSITE :

USERNAME :

PASSWORD :

NOTE :

WEBSITE :

USERNAME :

PASSWORD :

NOTE :

WEBSITE :

USERNAME :

PASSWORD :

NOTE :

WEBSITE :

USERNAME :

PASSWORD :

NOTE :

WEBSITE :

USERNAME :

PASSWORD :

NOTE :

T

WEBSITE :

USERNAME :

PASSWORD :

NOTE :

WEBSITE :

USERNAME :

PASSWORD :

NOTE :

WEBSITE :

USERNAME :

PASSWORD :

NOTE :

WEBSITE :

USERNAME :

PASSWORD :

NOTE :

WEBSITE :

USERNAME :

PASSWORD :

NOTE :

WEBSITE :

USERNAME :

PASSWORD :

NOTE :

WEBSITE :

USERNAME :

PASSWORD :

NOTE :

WEBSITE :

USERNAME :

PASSWORD :

NOTE :

T

WEBSITE :

USERNAME :

PASSWORD :

NOTE :

WEBSITE :

USERNAME :

PASSWORD :

NOTE :

WEBSITE :

USERNAME :

PASSWORD :

NOTE :

WEBSITE :

USERNAME :

PASSWORD :

NOTE :

WEBSITE :

USERNAME :

PASSWORD :

NOTE :

WEBSITE :

USERNAME :

PASSWORD :

NOTE :

WEBSITE :

USERNAME :

PASSWORD :

NOTE :

WEBSITE :

USERNAME :

PASSWORD :

NOTE :

U

WEBSITE :

USERNAME :

PASSWORD :

NOTE :

WEBSITE :

USERNAME :

PASSWORD :

NOTE :

WEBSITE :

USERNAME :

PASSWORD :

NOTE :

WEBSITE :

USERNAME :

PASSWORD :

NOTE :

WEBSITE :

USERNAME :

PASSWORD :

NOTE :

WEBSITE :

USERNAME :

PASSWORD :

NOTE :

WEBSITE :

USERNAME :

PASSWORD :

NOTE :

WEBSITE :

USERNAME :

PASSWORD :

NOTE :

U

WEBSITE :

USERNAME :

PASSWORD :

NOTE :

WEBSITE :

USERNAME :

PASSWORD :

NOTE :

WEBSITE :

USERNAME :

PASSWORD :

NOTE :

WEBSITE :

USERNAME :

PASSWORD :

NOTE :

WEBSITE :

USERNAME :

PASSWORD :

NOTE :

WEBSITE :

USERNAME :

PASSWORD :

NOTE :

WEBSITE :

USERNAME :

PASSWORD :

NOTE :

WEBSITE :

USERNAME :

PASSWORD :

NOTE :

V

WEBSITE :

USERNAME :

PASSWORD :

NOTE :

WEBSITE :

USERNAME :

PASSWORD :

NOTE :

WEBSITE :

USERNAME :

PASSWORD :

NOTE :

WEBSITE :

USERNAME :

PASSWORD :

NOTE :

WEBSITE :

USERNAME :

PASSWORD :

NOTE :

WEBSITE :

USERNAME :

PASSWORD :

NOTE :

WEBSITE :

USERNAME :

PASSWORD :

NOTE :

WEBSITE :

USERNAME :

PASSWORD :

NOTE :

V

WEBSITE :

USERNAME :

PASSWORD :

NOTE :

WEBSITE :

USERNAME :

PASSWORD :

NOTE :

WEBSITE :

USERNAME :

PASSWORD :

NOTE :

WEBSITE :

USERNAME :

PASSWORD :

NOTE :

WEBSITE :

USERNAME :

PASSWORD :

NOTE :

WEBSITE :

USERNAME :

PASSWORD :

NOTE :

WEBSITE :

USERNAME :

PASSWORD :

NOTE :

WEBSITE :

USERNAME :

PASSWORD :

NOTE :

W

WEBSITE :

USERNAME :

PASSWORD :

NOTE :

WEBSITE :

USERNAME :

PASSWORD :

NOTE :

WEBSITE :

USERNAME :

PASSWORD :

NOTE :

WEBSITE :

USERNAME :

PASSWORD :

NOTE :

WEBSITE :

USERNAME :

PASSWORD :

NOTE :

//

WEBSITE :

USERNAME :

PASSWORD :

NOTE :

//

WEBSITE :

USERNAME :

PASSWORD :

NOTE :

//

WEBSITE :

USERNAME :

PASSWORD :

NOTE :

//

W

WEBSITE :

USERNAME :

PASSWORD :

NOTE :

WEBSITE :

USERNAME :

PASSWORD :

NOTE :

WEBSITE :

USERNAME :

PASSWORD :

NOTE :

WEBSITE :

USERNAME :

PASSWORD :

NOTE :

WEBSITE :

USERNAME :

PASSWORD :

NOTE :

WEBSITE :

USERNAME :

PASSWORD :

NOTE :

WEBSITE :

USERNAME :

PASSWORD :

NOTE :

WEBSITE :

USERNAME :

PASSWORD :

NOTE :

X

WEBSITE :

USERNAME :

PASSWORD :

NOTE :

WEBSITE :

USERNAME :

PASSWORD :

NOTE :

WEBSITE :

USERNAME :

PASSWORD :

NOTE :

WEBSITE :

USERNAME :

PASSWORD :

NOTE :

WEBSITE :

USERNAME :

PASSWORD :

NOTE :

WEBSITE :

USERNAME :

PASSWORD :

NOTE :

WEBSITE :

USERNAME :

PASSWORD :

NOTE :

WEBSITE :

USERNAME :

PASSWORD :

NOTE :

X

WEBSITE :

USERNAME :

PASSWORD :

NOTE :

WEBSITE :

USERNAME :

PASSWORD :

NOTE :

WEBSITE :

USERNAME :

PASSWORD :

NOTE :

WEBSITE :

USERNAME :

PASSWORD :

NOTE :

WEBSITE :

USERNAME :

PASSWORD :

NOTE :

//

WEBSITE :

USERNAME :

PASSWORD :

NOTE :

//

WEBSITE :

USERNAME :

PASSWORD :

NOTE :

//

WEBSITE :

USERNAME :

PASSWORD :

NOTE :

//

Y

WEBSITE :

USERNAME :

PASSWORD :

NOTE :

WEBSITE :

USERNAME :

PASSWORD :

NOTE :

WEBSITE :

USERNAME :

PASSWORD :

NOTE :

WEBSITE :

USERNAME :

PASSWORD :

NOTE :

WEBSITE :

USERNAME :

PASSWORD :

NOTE :

//

WEBSITE :

USERNAME :

PASSWORD :

NOTE :

//

WEBSITE :

USERNAME :

PASSWORD :

NOTE :

//

WEBSITE :

USERNAME :

PASSWORD :

NOTE :

//

Y

WEBSITE :

USERNAME :

PASSWORD :

NOTE :

WEBSITE :

USERNAME :

PASSWORD :

NOTE :

WEBSITE :

USERNAME :

PASSWORD :

NOTE :

WEBSITE :

USERNAME :

PASSWORD :

NOTE :

WEBSITE :

USERNAME :

PASSWORD :

NOTE :

WEBSITE :

USERNAME :

PASSWORD :

NOTE :

WEBSITE :

USERNAME :

PASSWORD :

NOTE :

WEBSITE :

USERNAME :

PASSWORD :

NOTE :

Z

WEBSITE :

USERNAME :

PASSWORD :

NOTE :

WEBSITE :

USERNAME :

PASSWORD :

NOTE :

WEBSITE :

USERNAME :

PASSWORD :

NOTE :

WEBSITE :

USERNAME :

PASSWORD :

NOTE :

WEBSITE :

USERNAME :

PASSWORD :

NOTE :

//

WEBSITE :

USERNAME :

PASSWORD :

NOTE :

//

WEBSITE :

USERNAME :

PASSWORD :

NOTE :

//

WEBSITE :

USERNAME :

PASSWORD :

NOTE :

//

Z

WEBSITE :

USERNAME :

PASSWORD :

NOTE :

WEBSITE :

USERNAME :

PASSWORD :

NOTE :

WEBSITE :

USERNAME :

PASSWORD :

NOTE :

WEBSITE :

USERNAME :

PASSWORD :

NOTE :

WEBSITE :

USERNAME :

PASSWORD :

NOTE :

WEBSITE :

USERNAME :

PASSWORD :

NOTE :

WEBSITE :

USERNAME :

PASSWORD :

NOTE :

WEBSITE :

USERNAME :

PASSWORD :

NOTE :

WEBSITE :

USERNAME :

PASSWORD :

NOTE :

WEBSITE :

USERNAME :

PASSWORD :

NOTE :

WEBSITE :

USERNAME :

PASSWORD :

NOTE :

WEBSITE :

USERNAME :

PASSWORD :

NOTE :

WEBSITE :

USERNAME :

PASSWORD :

NOTE :

WEBSITE :

USERNAME :

PASSWORD :

NOTE :

WEBSITE :

USERNAME :

PASSWORD :

NOTE :

WEBSITE :

USERNAME :

PASSWORD :

NOTE :

WEBSITE :

USERNAME :

PASSWORD :

NOTE :

WEBSITE :

USERNAME :

PASSWORD :

NOTE :

WEBSITE :

USERNAME :

PASSWORD :

NOTE :

WEBSITE :

USERNAME :

PASSWORD :

NOTE :

Made in United States
North Haven, CT
12 February 2024